Who Wins:

Science or Scripture?

Your Heart? Your Mind? Or Your Faith?

John Seah

For suggestions, feedback, training, speaking engagements, purchase of books, please write to Johnseah@everesti.com.

Disclaimer:

Much as we have taken steps to ensure the accuracy of the information shared in this book, the publisher and the author do not warrant that the information is complete and shall not be liable for any damages incurred as a result of its use.

Our stories involve purely fictional characters like Einstein, Moses and Darwin having meetings in a coffee shop in hypothetical scenarios. These are used in the book to make it more interesting and relatable. In no way, do they contribute to the interpretation of the Bible or science.

Dedicated to the three treasures in my life that God has blessed me with:

My wife: **Lynn Foo**

My children: **Seah Wen Da**

                Seah Wen Zhen

Acknowledgments to our reviewers:

A big thank you of cosmic proportion,

In the grand cosmic dance of writing and creation, no endeavour is truly solitary. It takes a constellation of stars to light the way and I have been blessed to have some of the brightest in my universe. To all those who have helped make this book possible, I offer my thanks and heartfelt gratitude.

To my Christian friends,

Your unwavering support and enthusiasm have been like rocket fuel propelling me forward. Your thoughtful critiques and cosmic brainstorming sessions have been a true gift. Thank you for being my cosmic co-pilots on this literary journey.

Ang, Chistine	Chen Jia Lin
Goh Eng Lian, Jessie	Goh Mei Ling, Mel
Lim, Elaine	Lim Kim Yang, Andre
Ng Shio Wei, Linda	Tan Quee Chew
Tan, Daniel	Wang, Luke David
Yee, William	

To my family and relatives,

You have been the orbiting moons of my creative process, exerting your gravitational pull to keep me on track. Your encouragement, your late-night conversations about the intricacies of science and faith and your willingness to debate and delve into the mysteries of the universe have been priceless.

You have patiently combed through drafts, untangled the cosmic knots of grammar and helped polish every word and phrase - I salute you. You have turned nebulous ideas into shining stars.

Lynn Foo

Sharene Foo

Cheryl Seah

With cosmic gratitude,

John Seah

Who is This Book for?

Our target readers:

This book has been carefully crafted to cater to a diverse range of readers, each with their unique backgrounds, interests and perspectives. Its content is designed to resonate with and hopefully benefit the following groups of individuals:

1. **Atheists and Agnostics**: Since you are not sure if there is a God and we are embarking on a journey to answer that question, we invite you to explore with us, to have some light-hearted adventure, to enjoy some thought-provoking questions and humour along the way and perhaps together we can see some shimmering light at the end of our journey.

2. **Non-Christians and Pre-believers**: For those who have yet to embrace a faith or spiritual path or have embraced a different faith, this book serves as an open door to explore the world of Christian faith. It provides a welcoming and informative introduction to the Christian faith, allowing you to embark on a journey of self-discovery.

3. **2nd or 3rd Generation Christians**: It is an opportunity for you to explore what you have been imposed on and which you may have no interest in. Perhaps, this book may lead you to turn "mommy's or daddy's faith" into "my faith".

4. **Nerdy People**: Embracing a love for knowledge, this book invites individuals with an inclination towards intellectual pursuits to delve into the realm of faith and spirituality. It presents complex concepts in a way that appeals to the curious and analytical mind, providing an intellectual adventure.

5. **Curious Explorers**: For those who are naturally inquisitive and seek to uncover the mysteries of existence and the universe, this book offers a journey into the profound questions that have intrigued humanity for centuries. It encourages readers to embark on a quest for deeper understanding and meaning.

6. **Rational and Logical Thinkers**: Even individuals who prioritize reason and logic can find valuable insights within these pages. This book harmonizes faith with reason, offering a balanced perspective that allows rational thinkers to explore spirituality without compromising their intellectual integrity.

7. **Scientists, Engineers and Researchers**: The world of science, engineering and spirituality need not be at odds. This book bridges the gap between these seemingly disparate realms, enabling scientists to explore the spiritual dimension of life and existence in a way that aligns with their empirical and logical mindset.

8. **Muggles, Wizards and Witches**: Whether you are in the Harry Porter world or a muggle (ordinary people) world, whether you approach life with a grounded, down-to-earth perspective or have an affinity for the miraculous and extraordinary, this book engages both sides of the spectrum. It navigates the boundaries between the ordinary and the extraordinary, encouraging readers to explore the profound within the everyday.

9. **Successful People Who Feel That They Do Not Need God**: Success can sometimes lead to a sense of self-sufficiency. This book invites those who have achieved remarkable success to consider the spiritual aspects of their journey. It offers insights and reflections that can enhance their lives and provide a sense of purpose beyond material achievements. It also answers bigger questions which successful people ask, "Like why am I here? What is my purpose?" Perhaps this book can help you discover a bigger purpose beyond physical possessions and creature comforts.

10. **Christians Who Need a Nudge to do Something for Their Friends or Family Members**: May this book inspire you and make it easier for you to talk to them or simply pass this book on to them.

Einstein Humour 1

Einstein Humour 2

Moses Humour 1

Moses Humour 2

Contents

Chapter 1: A Playful Prelude

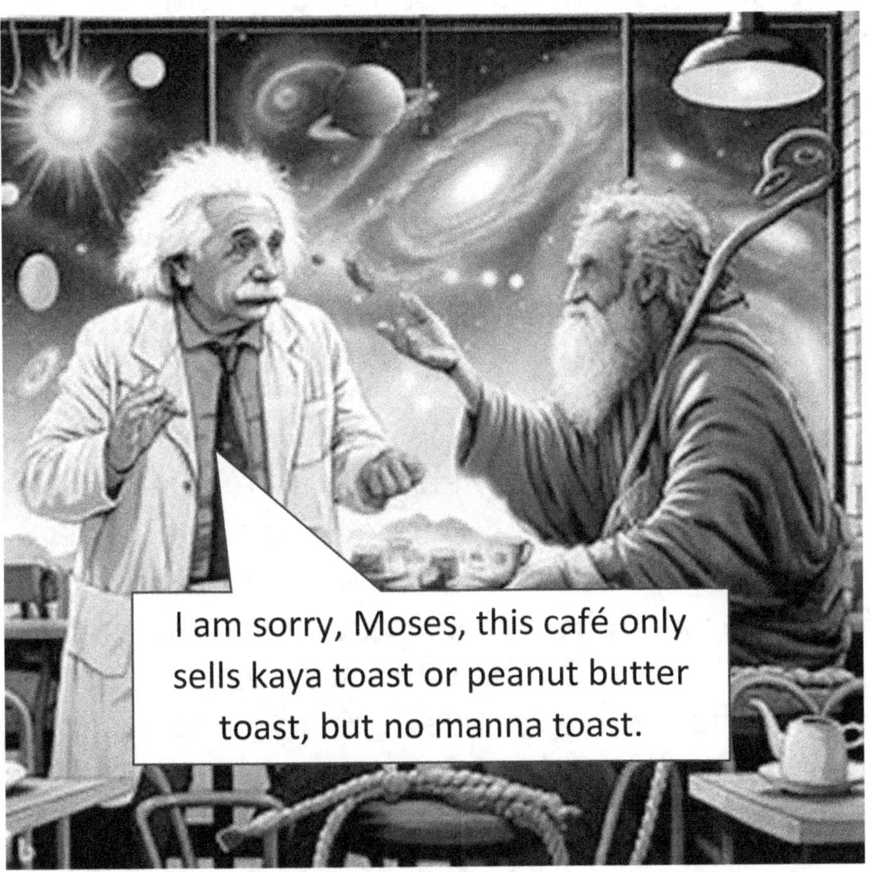

Chapter 1: A Playful Prelude

We embark on a journey through time, ideas and perspectives to explore whether science and the Bible are inter-galactical warring factions, rivals, companions or a pair of waltzing duo.

Who Won What? Your Heart? Your Mind? Or Your Faith?

Is this book about a petty argument or an eternal debate? Science is based on logical thinking and observable evidence. And faith in scripture is based on believing in God. Can scripture ever win your heart? Wanna explore…?

Our story began in a cozy coffee shop on a bustling corner of town. There were two friends who seemed an unlikely pair. On one side of the table sat Einstein, a man of science with a head full of equations and a mind bursting with curiosity. On the other side was Moses, an ancient theologian with a twinkle in his eye and wisdom etched into every line on his face.

In this book, Einstein is a persona that represents a character who is an expert in science.

Einstein was the sort of fellow who would take apart a clock just to see how it ticked and then try to make it tick better, tick louder or tick faster (oops!). He was known for his wild hair and even wilder ideas, a scientist who had explored the depths of the universe and the mysteries of time. Yet, despite all he knew about quarks, black holes and multiverse, there were still answers that eluded him.

Moses, on the other hand, had walked through the Red Sea and climbed mountains to find enlightenment. His journeys had taken him through the wilderness that many could only dream (or nightmares) of, both in the physical and the spiritual realm. He was a man who found wisdom in the ancient scrolls of the Scripture.

In this book, Moses is a persona that represents a character who is an expert in the Bible.

This fine day, as they sat sipping their lattes, Einstein decided to share a discovery that had been dancing through his thoughts. "You know, Moses," he began, "I've been pondering the nature of the universe. From my research, everything we see and know can be broken down into these three things: **time, space and matter."**

Moses, with a knowing look, took a thoughtful sip of his latte, as if he had a secret up his ancient sleeve. He grinned and leaned in closer to his friend, saying, "You know what's even more fascinating, my dear Einstein? The Bible knew that too!"

Einstein, ever the inquisitive one, raised an eyebrow and asked, "Really? How does the Bible fit into all of this?"

Moses cleared his throat and embarked on a wisdom-mode guru-style explanation. "Well, the Bible starts with this very first verse:

"In the beginning, God created the heavens and the earth."

Genesis 1:1, NIV

'In the beginning' means **time,**

'God created the heavens' means **space,**

'**And the earth'** that's **matter.**

"So, there you go, my friend; the first verse of the first chapter in the first book, Genesis, of the Bible tells us that God is the One who created the universe! God spoke and things came into being that were not there before."

Einstein was taken aback by this revelation. "Wow," he said with a chuckle, "that's a brilliant way to put it! I should read the Bible more often for answers to my scientific questions. It's like reading the front-page headline!"

1st book,

1st chapter,

1st verse!

"If only I had bothered to open my Bible, I would have obtained this answer in a second rather than to spend so many precious years on my research to come to the same conclusion!" Einstein thought to himself.

And with that, the stage was set for their grand adventure through the mysteries of science and the ancient secrets of the Bible. Little did they know that their light-hearted conversation in that coffee shop would lead to a journey filled with wonder, curiosity, and the ever-present possibility of a revelation waiting to unfold.

Chapter 2: In the Beginning - A Cosmic Coffee Shop Encounter

Chapter 2: In the Beginning - a Cosmic Coffee Shop Encounter

And so, dear reader, our cosmic journey begins with a delightful encounter over coffee - a meeting of great minds that hints at the possibility that science and faith may not be adversaries after all. Instead, they might just be cosmic companions, dancing in tandem to decipher the profound mysteries of existence.

As Einstein sipped his coffee, a newfound curiosity kindled within him. In that "wisdom-filled-to-the-rim" coffee shop encounter, he had glimpsed a bridge between science and faith, a path he had never considered before. As he gazed at the Bible and its ancient wisdom, he pondered the idea that perhaps the answers to his next scientific breakthrough lay not only in the explorations, equations and experiments in his lab but also in the psalms, proverbs and parables of this ancient Bible. With a wry smile, he made a silent resolution - to embark on a journey into the pages of the Bible, not as a theologian, but as a scientist seeking to unlock the universe's deepest mysteries.

Little did he know that this thought would lead him on a quest that would reshape his understanding of both science and spirituality.

Our tale unfolds, a journey where a thousand boundaries between science and faith merge and where a light-year of universe's secrets await discovery in the most unexpected of places.

A) The Big Bang Theory

In the midst of their ongoing dialogue, Einstein and Moses found themselves entangled in a spirited conversation about one of the most profound and revolutionary ideas in the history of science: **The Big Bang Theory**. The Big Bang Theory was originally proposed by the Belgian astronomer and physicist Georges Lemaître in the 1920s. The theory, like the story of Creation in the book of Genesis, aimed to unravel the mysteries of the universe's birth.

Einstein leaned forward, his unruly hair messing up the neat pattern on his cappuccino, and began, "Moses, you've shared your insights on Creation from Genesis, but there's something I'd like to explore with you. It's called the Big Bang Theory, and it's a theory of the universe's beginning from the scientific perspective."

Moses, with a warm and welcoming demeanour, nodded, signalling his readiness to engage. "I'm eager to hear more about this, my friend. Please, enlighten me."

Einstein explained, "The Big Bang Theory proposes that the universe as we know it began with an immense explosion. Before this event, the entire universe was condensed into an incredibly hot and dense state. Then, in a cosmic instant, it expanded and exploded with a big bang, leading to the formation of stars, galaxies and planets. The planets and stars are still moving away from each other as the galaxies expand. The theory proposes that the universe began as a singularity, a point of infinite density and extremely hot temperature.

Scientists observed that there was:

1)   an abundance of light elements during the immense explosion and that

2)   the universe is expanding and the planets, stars and galaxies are moving away from each other."

Moses listened intently, then with a contemplative smile, he said, "The Christian faith does not agree with the Big Bang Theory because we believe that God create the universe, but we are happy that science had detected evidence of 'an abundance of light elements' and an 'expanding universe' which agrees with the Bible. We do not believe that the universe began with a very dense massive point.

"It's fascinating, Einstein. Some part of this scientific theory indeed echoes the idea of creation as described in Genesis. The 'abundance of light detected' could be at the very instance when God spoke:

"And God said, 'Let there be light,' and there was light."   ***Genesis 1:3 NIV***

"I can quote several verses in the Bible where 'stretches out the heavens' can be interpreted as the expanding universe."

"He alone stretches out the heavens and treads on the waves of the sea."   **Job 9:8 NIV**

"The Lord wraps himself in light as with a garment; he stretches out the heavens like a tent."

Psalm 104:2 NIV

"…The LORD, who stretches out the heavens, who lays the foundation of the earth, and who forms the human spirit within a person…"

Zechariah 12:1 NIV

Einstein continued, "Exactly, Moses. The Big Bang Theory has brought science closer to understanding the universe's origin. Science today is not advanced enough to detect the presence of God or God's creation powers. It merely offers a scientific explanation of how the universe came about from its earliest moments based on observable and detectable evidence."

Moses responded thoughtfully, "I appreciate your perspective. It seems that both science and spirituality, far from being adversaries, can enrich our understanding of existence."

Their conversation meandered through the ages, touching on the harmony between scientific inquiry and spiritual reflection. The modern Big Bang Theory, despite its mind-boggling complexity, became another piece in the puzzle of understanding the universe.

As they concluded their discussion for the day, Einstein gazed out the window, pondering the vastness of the cosmos. Deep in thought, he murmured, "Why haven't I consider the Bible's Creation Story? Perhaps I need to research deeper into this perspective…"

Moses, on the other hand, contemplated the wisdom of ancient texts. Both found solace in the idea that their conversations were like stars illuminating the sky of understanding, revealing the profound connection between modern science and ancient scripture.

And so, they continued their delightful and harmonious exploration, embarking on each new topic with the joy of discovery and the hope of unravelling more of the universe's deep and intricate secrets.

B)   The Earth Floats in Space

Einstein, always eager to highlight the marvels of modern science, recalled that ancient sailors were afraid to sail far off from shores because they were afraid of falling off the edge of the earth. He chuckled as he tried to impress this ancient man in front of him with modern scientific knowledge. He wanted to impress Moses with this fact - that modern science discovered in 1640 AD that the Earth floats in space, seemingly suspended by an unseen force.

Moses, however, had a knowing smile on his face as he leaned in and remarked, "My dear Einstein, we've known that for thousands of years." With a twinkle in his ancient eyes, he quoted a verse from the Book of Job, written in the sixth century BC:

"He spreads out the northern skies over empty space; he suspends the earth over nothing."

Job 26:7 NIV

It was a poetic yet profound verse that hinted at a deep understanding of Earth's place in the universe - a wisdom that had been captured in scripture thousands of years before modern science caught up.

C)   The Earth is Round

Not one to be outdone, Einstein decided to delve into the subject of the Earth's shape, aware of the centuries-old myth that the world was flat and that ships would sail off the edge. He passionately explained that science had proven the Earth is round, emphasizing that ships do not plunge off the cliff but rather follow the curvature of the planet.

Moses, with his unshakable wisdom, simply nodded and responded, "You see, my friend, the Bible recognizes this truth as well." He quoted from the Book of Isaiah, a verse that affirmed Earth's spherical nature:

"He sits enthroned above the circle of the earth, ..."

Isaiah 40:22 NIV

In these ancient words, Einstein found affirmation of what modern science had confirmed only thousands of years later, after the Bible was written.

D)   Drawing Blood from Patients to Diagnose Diseases

As the conversation continued to weave between science and scripture, Einstein turned his attention to the field of medicine. He marvelled at the advancements of modern medicine, particularly the practice of drawing blood from patients to diagnose diseases. He considered it a testament to the precision of medical science in understanding the human body.

Once again, Moses responded with a calm assurance, "Einstein, my friend, we are aware of this principle millennia ago." He pointed to a verse from the Book of Leviticus, written in ancient times:

"For the life of a creature is in the blood, ..."

Leviticus 17:11 NIV

It was a statement that not only acknowledged the importance of blood in sustaining life but also hinted at its role in diagnosing ailments, an insight that predated the scientific understanding of blood's vital significance.

As their conversation continued to bridge the gap between the ancient wisdom of scripture and the modern discoveries of science, Einstein could not help but be struck by the profound insights contained within the Bible. He realized that the intersection of science and faith held untold treasures waiting to be unearthed and he felt a growing appreciation for the wisdom that had endured for millennia within those sacred texts. This chance encounter over coffee was turning into a journey of enlightenment and revelation, with the boundaries between the two realms becoming increasingly merged.

Summary

Scientific Discovery	Year Discovery was Made	Bible Verse	Year Book was Written	Gap Between Science and Bible
Evidence of:		Genesis 1:1 - "In the beginning..."		
Abundance of light elements	1927	Genesis 1:3 - "Let there be light..." Job 9:8, Psalm 104:2 & Zech 12:1	~1400 BCE	~3327 years ahead
Expanding galaxies		"… stretches out the heavens…"		
Earth Floats in Space	1650	Job 26:7 – "he suspends the earth over nothing…"	~1400 BCE	~3,050 years ahead
Earth is Round	4th Century BCE	Isaiah 40:22 - "He sits enthroned above the circle of the earth..."	~740 BCE	~1,100 years ahead
Blood Tests in Medicine	20th Century	Leviticus 17:11 - "For the life of a creature is in the blood, …"	~1445 BCE	~3,400 years ahead

Questions to Ponder:

1.   Can you think of any rational explanations how these four biblical book authors (Genesis, Isaiah, Job and Leviticus) were able to write about these discoveries thousands of years ahead of modern scientists' discoveries?

a.   The detected evidence of "abundance of light" and

b.   "Expanding universe" is aligned with the scriptures in the Bible.

c.   The earth floats in space "he suspends the earth over nothing…"

d.   The earth is round "He sits enthroned above the circle of the earth..."

e.   "For the life of a creature is in the blood, …"

2.   Could these be voices from God above?

3.   In the Big Bang Theory, where does the initial "very dense matter" come from, if there is no God to create it?

Let us explore more…☐

Chapter 3: When Science Meets Scriptures

Chapter 3: When Science Meets Scriptures

The next day, Einstein could hardly contain his excitement as he prepared to meet with Moses once again. Their previous discussion had left him yearning for more revelations hidden within the ancient texts of the Bible - a book that occupied a prominent place on his bookshelf in his living room but never opened. Never in his heart, never in his mind.

With a quick exchange of greetings, they settled into their conversation, ready to embark on another exciting journey of discovery.

Moses began by alluding to a verse in the Bible:

"All streams flow into the sea, yet the sea is never full. To the place the streams come from, there they return again."

Ecclesiastes 1:7, NIV

He pointed out the inherent wisdom in this passage, which suggested a cycle of evaporation and condensation, a concept essential **to understanding the Earth's water cycle.**

Einstein was intrigued. "The water cycle? It's fascinating to think that the Bible might have hinted at such a fundamental natural process."

Moses nodded, "Indeed, it appears that the ancient writers had a keen sense of observation and an understanding of the world around them. They recognized the perpetual movement of water from the Earth to the sky and back again. That ancient writer was our King Solomon, the wisest king that ever lived."

Einstein leaned forward, eager for more. "What else does the Bible hold in its pages?"

Moses continued, "Astronomy also finds its place in the Bible. References to **stars and constellations** can be found in Job 38:31, where it speaks of the Pleiades and Orion. The book of Psalms (Psalm 147:4) even attributes the naming of stars to God Himself."

"Can you bind the chains of the Pleiades? Can you loosen Orion's belt?"

Job 38:31 NIV

"He determines the number of the stars and calls them each by name."

Psalm 147:4 NIV

Einstein's eyes sparkled with curiosity. "Stars and constellations - astronomy was clearly a subject of interest in the ancient world."

As their conversation flowed, Moses shared more intriguing insights: "**Hygiene and quarantine practices**, as seen in Leviticus 13-15, demonstrate an early understanding of infectious diseases. It describes the process of isolation and washing of hands to prevent the spreading of infectious diseases."

"Amazing," said Einstein, "modern scientists only discover about micro-organism in 1665, and Leviticus was written in 1400BC. The Bible already instructed the people about hygiene and quarantine practices, three thousand years ahead of modern science!"

37 "Jacob, however, took fresh-cut branches from poplar, almond and plane trees and made white stripes on them by peeling the bark and exposing the white inner wood of the branches. 38 Then he placed the peeled branches in all the watering troughs, so that they would be directly in front of the flocks when they came to drink. When the flocks were in heat and came to drink, 39 they mated in front of the branches. And they bore young that were streaked, speckled, or spotted. 40 Jacob set apart the young of the flock by themselves, but made the rest face the streaked and dark-coloured animals that belonged to Laban. Thus, he made separate flocks for himself and did not put them with Laban's animals. 41 Whenever the stronger females were in heat, Jacob would place the branches in the troughs in front of the animals so they would mate near the branches, 42 but if the animals were weak, he would not place them there. So, the weak animals went to Laban and the strong ones to Jacob. 43 In this way the man grew exceedingly prosperous and came to own large flocks, and female and male servants, and camels and donkeys."

Genesis 30:37-43 NIV

"Genetic principles akin to early heredity concepts can be found **in Jacob's selective breeding of livestock**."

"I know," said Moses, "Jacob's breeding experiment with the striped and spotted goats was an attempt to increase his wealth and build up his own flock. By selectively breeding the goats that had the desired traits, Jacob was able to acquire a large number of animals with valuable markings."

Einstein leaned back, his mind racing with thoughts. "Early genetics and health practices in the Bible! It's like re-discovering ancient scientific knowledge three thousand years after it was written in the Bible!"

"This is mind-blowing! I am fascinated to learn that, despite all our great modern scientific minds and instruments, the Bible already taught us how to deal with the spreading of diseases caused by germs and viruses, something that we cannot see! But, but how…did the author know these things…?" Einstein struggled to put his thoughts together.

"That's because, as I have told you earlier, the Bible has a divine editor!" Moses said wisely. "Such thoughts and revelations come from God, not the human authors."

Moses concluded with a grin, "And let's not forget geology and tectonics. Psalm 104:32 describes the earth shaking. It's as if the Bible hints at geological phenomena."

"He who looks at the earth, and it trembles, who touches the mountains, and they smoke."

Psalm 104:32 NIV

"I don't understand this verse." said Einstein.

"In this verse, God is telling you about his power and majesty," explained Moses.

Einstein nodded in appreciation. "Moses, you've opened my eyes to the profound wisdom hidden within the Bible's pages. It's not merely a religious text but a treasure trove of ancient knowledge waiting to be unearthed. And possible proofs of God's existence!"

Moses smiled warmly, "Indeed, my friend. The Bible holds the secrets that bridge the gap between ancient wisdom and modern understanding. It's a testament to the enduring relevance of its teachings."

Their conversation continued, taking them on an extraordinary journey of discovery. Einstein and Moses found themselves exploring the remarkable intersection of ancient wisdom and science, a realm where the past and the present harmonized in a symphony of enlightenment and knowledge.

Summary Table

Scientific Discovery	Bible Verse	Year the Book is Written	Year Modern Science Discovery was Made	Gap between Science and Bible
Water Cycle	Ecclesiastes 1:7 - "All streams flow into the sea, yet the sea is never full..."	~935 BCE	17th Century	~2,600 years ahead
Discovery of Pleiades and Orion's belt	Job 38:31 - References to stars and constellations	~1440 BCE	Galileo Galilei was the first astronomer to view the Pleiades through a telescope. He thereby discovered that the cluster contains many stars too dim to be seen with the naked eye	3050 years ahead

			in 1610	
Hygiene and Quarantine	Leviticus 13-15 - Instructions for dealing with infectious diseases	~1445 BCE	Development of modern hygiene practices 1377 in Dubrovnik	2822 years ahead
Genetics and Heredity	Genesis 30:37-43 - Jacob's selective breeding of livestock	~1445 BCE	Early understanding of genetics 1725 – 1795	3000 years ahead
Geology and Tectonics	Psalm 104:32 - "He who looks at the earth, and it trembles..."	~1000 BCE	Development of modern geology, James Hutton (1726–1797), a Scottish farmer and naturalist, is known as the founder of modern geology	2726 years ahead

Questions to Ponder:

1.   How would these Bible authors (Ecclesiastes, Job, Leviticus, Genesis, Psalm) have known and wrote these science facts three thousand years ahead of modern scientists?

2.   Could they have heard some divine whispers? Or had divine handholding?

Don't all these facts confirm that the Bible is a product of 40 human authors, inspired and coordinated by one divine editor? ☐

Chapter 4: Is the Bible Divine Wisdom or Human Handiwork?

Chapter 4: Is the Bible Divine Wisdom or Human Handiwork?

The coffee shop had become a nexus of conversation, a place where two great minds, one of science and one of faith, found common ground amid the rich aroma of freshly brewed coffee. Einstein, with his characteristic curiosity, was now diving into the depths of the Bible's wisdom, a tome he had never explored in such detail before.

Einstein could not contain his fascination. "Moses," he began, "I've been reading the Bible, and I must admit, I'm astounded by the depth of wisdom contained within its pages. But tell me, which wise ancient thinker could have possessed such foresight? Who among them could have known so much about the future?"

Moses, the sage of antiquity, offered a serene smile. He leaned in and responded, "My dear Einstein, that's the very question that has intrigued minds for centuries. You see, the Bible is not just the work of human authors, but it's a divine tapestry woven across the annals of time. It is the Word of God, not mere man."

With the weight of millennia behind his words, Moses shared some remarkable facts about the Bible. "Consider this," he said, "the Bible is not a single book, but a compilation of 66 books, penned by 40 human authors across 1500 years, and in vastly different times and places. These ancient authors, separated by time and distance, had no means of direct communication with one another. Yet, their writings formed a coherent narrative, inspired by a divine editor - the hand of God."

The Bible is diverse; it is written by 40 different authors of different background, social status, educational level, time and culture, writing styles, passions and objectives, yet it is unified in:

- ☐ scientific facts

- ☐ moral instructions

- ☐ social behaviours

- ☐ historical facts

- ☐ archaeological insights

- ☐ medical wisdom

- ☐ geographical accuracy

- ☐ spiritual worship rituals

Einstein raised an eyebrow, intrigued by this notion. Moses continued, "The Bible contains an astonishing array of knowledge. It offers wisdom often centuries ahead of modern scientific discoveries. These revelations were not mere human insights but divine revelations to guide humanity."

The ancient sage leaned back, his eyes glinting with conviction. "Furthermore," Moses added, "today, there are over 1000 scrolls and historical records that historians have used to verify the authenticity and accuracy of the Bible's events. They are either with private collectors or in museums for all to see."

The Bible gives details like people, period, place so that the events can also be cross-referenced with non-biblical documents, such as written works from those periods and kings' palace records, artefacts, photos and video recordings. Examples are:

1. see www.ronwyatt.com
    Ron Wyatt Discoveries [2022] Gomorrah, Red Sea Crossing, Mt Sinai, Noah's Ark, Blood of Christ

    a. The presence of sulphur balls (brimstones) in the sites of Sodom and Gomorrah

    b. Discovery of Noah's Ark

    c. Red Sea crossing

    d. The Ark of the Covenant

    e. Blood of Jesus

2. See Institute of Creation Research website

    https://discoverycenter.icr.org/

All these external documents verified the correctness and validity of the biblical events and its stories.

Einstein, who had dedicated his life to unravelling the mysteries of the universe, found himself drawn into the enigma of the Bible's prophetic revelations. Moses spoke of the Bible encompassing the past, the present, and the future, with 735 prophesies about the future alone. "By your time, Einstein," Moses revealed, "81% of these prophesies have already come to pass. Christians believe with unwavering faith that the remaining 19% (mainly in the book of Revelation) will also be fulfilled. Let me give you some examples of prophecies about the first coming of Jesus Christ below." (See David Pawson website reference.)

Moses added "The Bible tells us that the Holy Spirit inspired the authors…"

"All Scripture is God-breathed and is useful for teaching, rebuking, correcting and training in righteousness, 17 so that the servant of God may be thoroughly equipped for every good work."

2 Timothy 3:16-17 NIV

As the conversation unfolded, Einstein realized that the Bible was not just a dusty relic of the past but a profound roadmap that spanned across the ages - a guide to the cosmos of existence, both seen and unseen. The notion that these revelations transcended human comprehension and were a testament to divine wisdom left him pondering the cosmic mysteries of faith and reason. The coffee shop, once just a place for casual conversation, had become the gateway to a journey that promised to illuminate the very fabric of existence itself.

Summary

Facts about the Bible:

A compilation of 66 books

Written by 40 human authors,

a.   separated by time (1500 years from the 1st book to the last book)

b.   separated by geographical space (thousands of kilometres apart)

c.   diversified by culture, profession, social status, writing styles

d.   yet unified in content and thoughts in these aspects:

1.   scientific facts

2.   moral instructions

3.   social behaviours

4.   historical facts

5.   archaeological insights

6.   medical wisdom

7.   geographical accuracy

8.   spiritual worship rituals

The Bible is verifiable by modern day experts like historians and archaeologists, that it has not been modified. It is authenticated by more than 1000 scrolls stored in museums and with private collectors, which modern day sceptics can read. It is written in Greek, Hebrew, and Aramaic. The events written in the Bible can be authenticated with events written in non-biblical books during those periods.

Examples of Prophecies about Jesus' 1st coming	Bible Reference	Estimated Period Written	Fulfilment by Jesus	Years Ahead of fulfilment
a. Born in Bethlehem	Micah 5:2	8th century BC	Matthew 2:1-6	Around 700
b. Virgin Birth	Isaiah 7:14	8th century BC	Matthew 1:18-25	Around 800
c. Messiah's Lineage	Genesis 49:10	15th century BC	Matthew 1:1-16	Around 1,500
d. Suffering and Rejection	Isaiah 53:3	8th century BC	New Testament	Around 800
e. Triumphal Entry	Zechariah 9:9	5th century BC	Matthew 21:1-11	Around 500
f. Crucifixion	Psalm 22:16-18	10th century BC	New Testament	Around 1,000

Examples of Prophecies about Jesus' 1st coming	Bible Reference	Estimated Period Written	Fulfilment by Jesus	Years Ahead of fulfilment
g. Resurrection	Psalm 16:10	10th century BC	New Testament	Around 1,000

Questions to ponder:

1. Can you think of any logical explanation how these 40 human authors can achieve such complex coordination, collaboration, and synchronization across 1600 years of time and thousands of kilometres of geographical distance without divine help?

2. Who gave them the wisdom to write science facts that would be discovered thousands of years ahead of modern scientists?

3. How can hundreds of prophesies, written hundreds of years ahead be fulfilled later exactly as prophesied?

What do you think? Is the Bible of human handiwork or of divine origin?

Let us explore on…

Chapter 5: Evolution vs. Creation: Does your Grandmother Look Like an Ape?

Chapter 5: Evolution vs. Creation: Does your Grandmother Look Like an Ape?

The cozy coffee shop, steeped in the aroma of freshly brewed coffee and the murmur of lively conversations, welcomed an unexpected guest this windy cool day. It was none other than Darwin.

Darwin, in our book, is a persona of a character who is an expert in the Theory of Evolution.

With polite greetings exchanged, the trio - Einstein, Darwin and Moses, settled around a table, their contrasting views on the origin of life creating an electrifying atmosphere. Besides the brewing coffee, a wind of change was also brewing.

Einstein, ever the man of science, initiated the discussion. "Darwin," he began, "it's a pleasure to have you here. We've been immersed in the fascinating world of modern science and the ancient Bible."

Darwin, with an air of composure, replied, "Thank you, Einstein. I'm intrigued by your discoveries, but I must share my perspective - the theory of evolution, which has transformed our understanding of life's complexities."

And thus, the grand debate unfolded, a cosmic and terrestrial clash of ideas.

Einstein, fortified with a wealth of scientific knowledge, presented his arguments:

A) Darwin's Theory of Evolution Cannot Be Considered as Science

"Darwin," Einstein said, "your theory is often critiqued for relying on assumptions drawn from sporadic fossil discoveries. It's a theory that cannot be tested or replicated, as it spans changes occurring over the vast expanse of billions of years. It cannot be experiment upon, it cannot be verified. It's not science. I say again, it's not science."

B) Law of Natural Adaptation

"In your research, Darwin, you had made a remarkable observation concerning the inhabitants of certain islands. One island was inhabited solely by finches with short, robust beaks, while another island was inhabited exclusively by finches with long, slender beaks. Darwin, you posited that these distinctive beak morphologies had arisen through evolutionary adaptation to their respective environments.

"However, let us entertain a hypothetical scenario in which both islands originally hosted finch populations with a mixture of beak types. On one of these islands, an abundance of nuts with thick shells presented a challenge, necessitating strong short beaks to access their contents. Consequently, finches with strong short beaks thrived, while their long-beaked counterparts struggled to obtain sustenance and perished. Conversely, on the other island, a profusion of insects concealed beneath tree bark favoured finches equipped with long, slender beaks capable of reaching these hidden delicacies. In this environment, finches with short beaks found themselves ill-suited and consequently faced extinction.

"This perspective reveals that your initial conclusion is wrong. Rather than the beaks themselves evolving, it is the survival and proliferation of finches possessing the most advantageous traits for their specific ecological niches that ultimately shape these populations. In essence, survival favours those species whose traits align with the demands of their environment."

"My conclusion," said Einstein, "is that these finches' beaks did not evolve. Those with the wrong traits cannot find food, therefore they died or became extinct."

C)   Theory of Evolution Does Not Account for How New Species are Created

"Your theory," he emphasized, "mainly addresses variations within the same species but leaves unanswered questions about the emergence of entirely new species. The discovery of chromosomes, each species with its unique count, challenges your notion of inter-species evolution. If dogs do not evolve to become wolves, where do wolves come from then?"

D) Theory of Evolution is Obsoleted by the Discovery of Chromosomes

What Is a Chromosome?

Imagine chromosomes as tiny books found inside your cells. These books are like instruction manuals for your body. Just like how you might have different books for different subjects, your cells have different chromosomes. They tell your body how to grow, what colour your hair and eyes should be, and many other things.

In your body, you have pairs of chromosomes, and one half of each pair comes from your mom, and the other half from your dad. This is why children look like their parents. These pairs make sure that when your body makes new cells or babies, they get the right instructions to work correctly. So, chromosomes are like the books with all the important rules, instructions and plans for your body.

What Is DNA?

Now, think of DNA as the special ink used to write in those instruction manuals (chromosomes). DNA is a long, twisty chain, like a very tiny ladder. It is made up of four different letters: A, T, C, and G. These letters are like the alphabet in a secret code that only your body can read.

Each "rung" on the ladder is made of two of these letters, like A with T or C with G. These rungs spell out the instructions for building and running your body. They decide if you will have curly hair, if your eyes will be brown or blue and many other things.

So, chromosomes are the instruction manuals in your cells, and DNA is the special ink that writes down those instructions. Together, they make sure your body knows how to be "you" and do all the amazing things it does.

"Furthermore," Einstein pointed out, "Darwin's theory which was published in 1859 is obsoleted by the discovery of chromosomes in 1955, a key omission.

It does not account for the effect of chromosomes. For instance:

1.   apes have 48 chromosomes,

2.   monkeys have 42 chromosomes, and

3.   humans have 46 distinct chromosome counts,

making inter-species evolution impossible. Therefore, human does not and cannot evolve from apes nor monkeys!"

E)   DNA Discovery Also Obsoleted the Theory of Evolution

"The discovery of DNA," Einstein continued, "casts further doubt on the theory of evolution. Consider the human DNA, with its three billion pairs of bases. The probability of random evolution successfully crafting these intricate sequences is staggeringly low. It's akin to recruiting a bunch of monkeys to hammer randomly on the keyboards, trying to hack the code of an Android phone, hoping it will, by some random chance, evolve into an iPhone over time."

F)   Time Freeze Experiment

"Lastly," Einstein "let us conduct an experiment. Let's stop time and evolution right here and right now. If evolution were true, all creatures on earth will be continually evolving with a few bits of DNA being modified at any one time, we'd expect billions of partially evolved or mutated creatures amongst us. Yet, all the humans, cats, dogs, insects, birds, and fishes remain 100% representative of their respective species. What halted the continual evolution process?

"The lack of billions of partially evolved or mutated creatures around the globe proved that the theory of evolution is not correct. There is no creature evolving at one or a few bits at a time over billions of years.

"The fact that all the billions of creatures around the world are running, hopping swimming, and flying perfectly means that their original billion-letter code remained perfect, the same as the day they were created. There is no evolution!"

Moses, steeped in ancient wisdom, interjected. "Einstein has raised many valid points, Darwin. The Bible teaches that all creatures are not products of randomness but creations by an intelligent designer - God. This perspective has resonated with countless people across millennia. Perhaps the answers to life's profound mysteries lie not in gradual evolution but in the meticulous design of a divine creator."

The atmosphere in the coffee shop was clearer now, with the mist of evolution vapourised. In the end, both Moses and Einstein emerged triumphant, their views resonating as the final word - the belief that we are all intelligently designed and purposefully created. Darwin's Theory of Evolution is, well… gone with the wind.

Darwin sighed. He knew that the Theory of Evolution had been proven wrong. So, he gathered his things and scurried out of the coffee shop liked a frightened lizard that had just lost its tail.

Summary

The Theory of Evolution (published in 1859) has been debunked for the following reasons:

A)   Theory of Evolution is not science.

B)   Law of Natural Adaptation is flawed.

C)   Theory of Evolution does not account for how new species are created.

D)   Theory of Evolution is made obsolete by the discovery of chromosomes by Walther Flemming in 1882

E)   Theory of Evolution is made obsolete by the discovery of DNA in 1860 by Swiss chemist Friedrich Miescher

F)   Time Freeze Experiment does not reveal any partially evolved creatures.

Therefore, believing in the theory of evolution is equivalent to believing that the sun revolves around the earth, or the earth is the centre of the universe. It's an obsolete theory!

Questions to Ponder...

If the Theory of Evolution is obsolete

1. Who created the first life on earth?

2. Who created the first human on Earth?

3. Who created the earth? Or the whole universe?

As stated in the Bible Genesis 1:1, "God created the heavens and the earth" and everything in it, including the first man and woman, Adam and Eve.

Is a divine creator a more logical explanation now than a random chaotic evolution?

If so, you are beautifully and purposely created!

Chapter 6: The Dawn of the Dinosaurs

Chapter 6: The Dawn of the Dinosaurs

Einstein, still buzzing with excitement from their previous discussions, couldn't help but wear a mischievous grin as he delved into yet another topic that had intrigued him. He leaned forward and with a playful twinkle in his eyes, asked, "Moses, my friend, what about the dinosaurs? Those colossal creatures that roamed the Earth a long, long time ago. Did the Bible have any hints about them too?"

Moses chuckled at Einstein's enthusiasm and replied, "You have quite the appetite for knowledge, my friend. The Bible doesn't explicitly mention dinosaur because no human has seen it yet, so we have no name for it in the Bible. However, the Bible does provide some intriguing clues about the Earth's ancient history."

Einstein leaned in closer, eager to hear more. "Clues? Tell me more!"

Moses began, "Let's consider the book of Genesis, which tells the Creation Story. God made the wild animals, the livestock and all the creatures that move along the ground according to their kinds."

"And God said, "Let the land produce living creatures according to their kinds: the livestock, the creatures that move along the ground, and the wild animals, each according to its kind." And it was so. God made the wild animals according to their kinds, the livestock according to their kinds, and all the

creatures that move along the ground according to their kinds. And God saw that it was good."

Genesis 1:24-25 NIV

Einstein pondered these verses. "So, the Bible mentions God creating creatures according to their kinds. Could that imply the various species, including dinosaurs, were created separately?"

Moses nodded, "Exactly, my friend. While the Bible doesn't name the dinosaurs explicitly, it suggests that various creatures were created 'according to their kinds.' This leaves room for the possibility that dinosaurs were among the creatures created in their own unique forms."

Einstein was intrigued by the idea. "It's a fascinating perspective. The Bible doesn't provide all the details, but it hints at the diversity of life on Earth."

Moses continued, "Indeed! When we consider the immense timescale involved in Earth's history, it's humbling. Dinosaurs, as you mentioned, lived millennia ago and the Bible offers a glimpse into the ancient tapestry of our planet's past."

Einstein couldn't help but be amazed. "3500 years ago, the Bible hinted at the diversity of life on Earth, including creatures that we've only recently discovered through palaeontology."

Moses smiled warmly, "The Bible's wisdom spans the ages and it continues to inspire awe and wonder as we uncover the mysteries of our world. It's a testament to the enduring relevance of its teachings."

As their conversation continued, Einstein and Moses marvelled at the Bible's ability to offer glimpses into the distant past, fostering a profound appreciation for the wonders of our planet's history, including the enigmatic reign of the dinosaurs that had captivated human imagination for centuries. As their conversation about the Bible and dinosaurs continued, Moses suddenly remembered a passage that might shed more light on the topic. He turned to Einstein with a curious expression and said, "Einstein, there's an intriguing passage about a creature called Behemoth, in the book of Job that has often been interpreted as a possible description of a dinosaur. It's found in Job 40:15-24."

Einstein leaned in, eager to hear more. " Behemoth? Tell me about it."

"Look at Behemoth,

which I made along with you

and which feeds on grass like an ox.

[16] *What strength it has in its loins,*

what power in the muscles of its belly!

[17] *Its tail sways like a cedar;*

the sinews of its thighs are close-knit.

[18] *Its bones are tubes of bronze,*

its limbs like rods of iron.

[19] *It ranks first among the works of God,*

yet its Maker can approach it with his sword.

²⁰ The hills bring it their produce,

and all the wild animals play nearby.

²¹ Under the lotus plants it lies,

hidden among the reeds in the marsh.

²² The lotuses conceal it in their shadow;

the poplars by the stream surround it.

²³ A raging river does not alarm it;

it is secure, though the Jordan should surge against its mouth.

²⁴ Can anyone capture it by the eyes,

or trap it and pierce its nose?"

Job 40:15-24 NIV

Einstein furrowed his brow, deep in thought. "That's quite a vivid description. It does sound like a massive and powerful creature. This is definitely the description of a dinosaur!"

Moses nodded, "Many scholars and theologians have pondered that possibility. Some suggest that Behemoth might indeed be a reference to a hippopotamus or an elephant or a large prehistoric creature. The description of its tail swaying like a cedar and its limbs resembling rods of iron certainly evoke images of a colossal beast. It cannot refer to a hippopotamus or an elephant as both have small tails".

Einstein was intrigued by the notion. "If this is a reference to a dinosaur, it's remarkable that such descriptions were found in the Bible millennia before even human existed, millennia before modern scientists uncovered the fossils of these creatures in 1676 AD."

Moses agreed, "It's a testament to the richness of the Bible's wisdom and the way it offers glimpses into the natural world millennia before human existence. Whether Behemoth is indeed a dinosaur or another extraordinary creature, it's a reminder of the diverse life forms that have inhabited our planet over eons."

As their conversation continued, Einstein and Moses contemplated the possibility that the Bible might contain veiled references to ancient creatures like dinosaurs. The mysteries of Earth's history continued to unfold, leaving them with a profound sense of wonder and admiration for both science and ancient wisdom.

Einstein, ever the practical thinker, raised a valid point as they delved into the possible existence of creatures like dinosaurs in the ancient world. He leaned forward and inquired, "But wouldn't such colossal creatures wreak havoc in human villages, Moses?"

Moses, who had spent his life contemplating the mysteries of the Bible, offered a thoughtful response. "Indeed, that's a valid concern, Einstein. If creatures like Behemoth, which we suspect could be dinosaurs, roamed the Earth alongside humans, it would raise questions about their interaction with our ancestors."

With a knowing smile, Moses continued, "But remember, my friend, that the Bible often speaks of God's wisdom and divine order. It's said that 'God, in his wisdom, kills it all with his sword!' "

Einstein raised an eyebrow, intrigued by this notion. "So, you're saying that God, in his wisdom, maintain balance in the world by intervening when necessary?"

Moses nodded, "Precisely, Einstein. The Bible often portrays God as the ultimate arbiter of order and justice in the universe. If creatures like Behemoth posed a threat or disrupted the balance of life on Earth, it's believed that God would have acted to restore that balance, perhaps by removing such creatures from the equation."

Einstein could not help but marvel at the depth of wisdom contained within the Bible. "It's a fascinating perspective, Moses. The idea that divine intervention played a role in maintaining harmony on Earth, even in the presence of such formidable creatures, adds another layer of complexity."

Moses concluded, "Indeed, my friend. The Bible's teachings often remind us of the intricate interplay between the natural world and the divine. It's a reminder that there's always more to discover and understand, both in the realms of science and spirituality."

As their conversation continued, Einstein and Moses contemplated the delicate balance that might have existed in the ancient world, where God's wisdom was believed to have guided the course of nature, even in the face of awe-inspiring creatures like dinosaurs. It was this thought-provoking perspective that left them with a sense of reverence for the mysteries of the universe.

"It ranks first among the works of God,

yet its Maker can approach it with his sword."

Job 40:19 NIV

Einstein's eyes lit up with a newfound realization. "Ah!" he exclaimed, a sense of profound understanding washing over him, "God creates and God destroys to maintain nature's balance. So, **the meteorite that caused the extinction of dinosaurs**, it's not a random passing ball of fire; **it's the sword of God!"**

Moses nodded in agreement, his expression reflecting the same sense of revelation. "Yes," he added, "God creates and God destroys. He is the ultimate orchestrator of the universe's grand design. In the verse we discussed earlier, 'It ranks first among the works of God, yet its Maker can approach it with His sword,' it becomes clear that God's sovereignty extends over all of creation."

Einstein continued, "So, it's not just about the creation of life but also about maintaining the delicate balance of the natural world. God's divine wisdom guides both the birth and the end of creatures and species to ensure that harmony prevails."

Moses smiled, "Precisely, Einstein. It's a reminder that God is not only the Creator but also the Sustainer of all life. He reigns over the past, the present, and the future. The meteorite that you mentioned, which may have caused the extinction of dinosaurs, is part of the divine plan."

Their conversation had taken an awe-inspiring turn, as they contemplated the interplay between creation and destruction in the universe. It was a reminder that God's hands guide the course of nature and ensure that all things, even the most cataclysmic events, serve a greater purpose in maintaining the equilibrium of the world.

As they sat there, immersed in their discussion, Einstein and Moses found themselves humbled by the grandeur of the cosmos and the profound mysteries that both science and spirituality sought to unravel.

Summary

Chapter 6 explores the intriguing existence and extinction of dinosaurs in the Bible and the concept of divine creation and destruction in maintaining the natural order of the world. It is a thought-provoking chapter that highlights the intersection of science, spirituality and the mysteries of our planet's history.

Questions to Ponder:

1.   Who gave the author of the book of Job in the Bible, the wisdom to describe in detail about dinosaurs' existence:

a.   before the first human ever walked on earth?

b.   before modern scientists unearthed their first fossil?

2.   Who gave the authors of the Bible the wisdom to describe about dinosaurs' extinction, millennia before modern scientists even knew about their existence?

I personally believe that the above point to a divine creator. What about you?

A Prelude to Chapter 7: Einstein's Involvement with the Atomic Bomb

A Prelude to Chapter 7: Einstein's Involvement with the Atomic Bomb

Albert Einstein is a name synonymous with genius, his frizzy hair and thoughtful eyes serving as iconic symbols of intellect. Yet, during the tumultuous era of World War II, Einstein's brilliant mind found itself embroiled in a moral and scientific dilemma that would shape the course of history.

In the early 1930s, as the storm clouds of war gathered over Europe, the scientific community became increasingly aware of the potential immense power locked within the atom. Among the brightest minds exploring this enigma were physicists Leo Szilard and Enrico Fermi. Recognizing the catastrophic potential of nuclear weapons, Szilard approached Einstein, who was living in Princeton, New Jersey, in 1938. Szilard's letter warned of the implications of harnessing atomic energy for military purposes, inspiring Einstein to act.

Einstein, renowned for his pacifist views, had a sense of responsibility to humanity. He was initially hesitant about participating in military research but soon realized that his involvement could be the difference between a world in which nuclear weapons were advanced or left undeveloped. Thus, he lent his voice and prestige to the cause.

Einstein's dilemma was also a race against time between either Hitler having an atomic bomb first to win the WW II by bombing either Paris or London or

Washington, or the Allied powers having an atomic bomb first to win WW II by dropping it in Germany. However, Japan's involvement was an unexpected twist of fate by their surprised bombing of the Pearl Habor.

Einstein's famous equation, E=mc2, had revealed the connection between energy and mass, laying the theoretical groundwork for the atomic bomb. This equation would haunt him in the years to come. In 1939, following a series of landmark discoveries, most notably the splitting of the uranium atom by Otto Hahn and Fritz Strassmann, Szilard and Einstein drafted a letter to President Franklin D. Roosevelt, warning of the Nazi regime's potential to develop an atomic weapon. This letter initiated the Manhattan Project, a top-secret program dedicated to the development of atomic bombs.

Einstein's involvement in the Manhattan Project was primarily symbolic. He was a member of the project's advisory board and played no direct role in the bomb's construction. Still, his endorsement was instrumental in securing the resources needed for the massive scientific and engineering undertaking.

As the war raged on, Einstein's inner turmoil deepened. He had hoped that his involvement would prevent the use of the atomic bomb, or at least hasten the war's end. The fateful day came on July 16, 1945, when the first successful test of an atomic bomb, codenamed Trinity, occurred in the New Mexico desert. Einstein was not present, but he knew the world had entered a new, perilous era.

On August 6 and 9, 1945, two atomic bombs were dropped on Hiroshima and Nagasaki, respectively, by the United States, leading to Japan's surrender and the end of World War II. Einstein, who had initially supported the project for fear that Nazi Germany might develop the bomb first, was now deeply distressed by the loss of life.

In the post-war years, Einstein became an advocate for nuclear disarmament, realizing the grave danger posed by the proliferation of atomic weapons. His involvement in the Manhattan Project, though intended to prevent the Nazis from obtaining such devastating power, had unleashed a force that would forever alter the course of history.

Albert Einstein's role in the invention of nuclear bombs remains a complex and morally charged chapter in the annals of science. His enduring legacy serves as a reminder of the profound ethical questions that accompany scientific progress and the ever-present need for responsible stewardship of knowledge and power.

Chapter 7: Did the Bible Prophesize About Nuclear Bombs?

Chapter 7: Did the Bible Prophesize About Nuclear Bombs?

The coffee shop buzzed with the usual chatter as Albert Einstein sat across from Moses, engaged in a conversation that spanned centuries. The two unlikely companions had met a few months earlier, and their discussions often veered into the realms of science, scripture, and spirituality. Today was no different.

Einstein, his iconic hair framing his thoughtful eyes, leaned in, his curiosity piqued by a question that had been nagging at him. "Since God is the sovereign ruler of the past, current and future," he began, "did the Bible prophesize about the nuclear bombs?" It was a thought that has been haunting him since the bombing of Hiroshima in 1945.

Moses, clad in ancient attire that seemed out of place in the modern coffee shop, furrowed his brows. The term "nuclear bombs" was foreign to him, a relic from a distant future that had yet to unfold. "Nuclear bombs?" Moses questioned; his voice tinged with curiosity. "I am unfamiliar with this term. Could you explain it to me?"

Einstein nodded, realizing that he needed to bridge the gap between their eras. "Nuclear bombs are incredibly destructive weapons that harness the power of the atom to create explosions of unimaginable magnitude. They can level entire cities and cause widespread devastation."

Moses listened intently, his eyes betraying a mixture of astonishment and concern. "I see," he said, trying to grasp the concept. "Such power in the hands of humanity is a troubling thought. But, to your question, yes, there are two verses in the Bible that some interpret as prophecies related to such destructive forces."

Einstein's eyes lit up with intrigue. "Please, Moses, share them with me."

Moses leaned back, recalling verses from his ancient scrolls. "The first one is from the Book of Zechariah," he said.

"And this shall be the plague with which the Lord will strike all the peoples that wage war against Jerusalem: their flesh will rot while they are still standing on their feet, their eyes will rot in their sockets, and their tongues will rot in their mouths."

Zechariah 14:12 NIV

Einstein listened, his mind racing as he considered the eerie similarity between this verse and the effects of nuclear radiation. He mused, "That's indeed striking! Yes, nuclear is the only weapon known to humankind that can rot flesh, tongues and eyes while the soldiers are still standing."

"What is the other verse?" Einstein asked.

Moses continued, "The second verse is from the Second Epistle of Peter, Chapter 3, Verse 10."

***10** "But the day of the Lord will come like a thief. The heavens will disappear with a roar; the elements will be destroyed by fire, and the earth and everything done in it will be laid bare."*

2 Peter 3:10 NIV

Einstein nodded solemnly, recognizing the parallel between the destruction described in the verse and the cataclysmic power of a nuclear explosion. He noted that the key word to any nuclear scientist "the elements will be destroyed by fire" is a strong clue pointing to a nuclear explosion.

Einstein began, "To explain why, let me begin with the smallest basic structure - an atom. It is the smallest particle of an element that can exist. It consists of protons, neutrons and electrons.

"An element is a pure substance that cannot be broken down by chemical methods into simpler parts. For example, a piece of iron consists of millions of iron atoms in it. The number of neutrons, protons and electrons are exactly the same for each of the iron atom. Different elements have different number of protons, neutrons and electrons.

"Take an element like oxygen, it typically has 8 protons, 8 electrons and 8 neutrons. The element oxygen can be frozen to a liquid state at -218.4°C. It can boil off to become a vapour state at -183°C. But, for the oxygen element to be destroyed, its atoms need to be split by a nuclear explosion so that the oxygen atom no longer contains 8 protons, 8 neutrons and 8 electrons. Then it is no longer oxygen since it has been destroyed. It will then lose the properties of oxygen."

Einstein noted that the Bible used the specific word **elements** and not material which could be cloth or wood.

"The sovereign God is in control of everything, the past, the present and future. He knows everything. He inspires the Bible authors to write things in the Bible thousands of years ahead of time to let us know that He is an omniscient God," Moses continued.

As they sipped their coffee, the coffee shop's modern surroundings seemed to blur, and for a moment, Einstein and Moses were united by their quest for understanding, bridging the gap between their worlds through timeless questions and the timeless words of the Bible.

Indeed, the notion that ancient texts could contain references to modern inventions like the atom bombs is truly mind-boggling. It reminds us of the intricate tapestry woven by human understanding across the ages - a tapestry where threads of ancient wisdom and contemporary knowledge intertwine in unexpected ways. As we contemplate the mysteries of these connections, we are reminded that the pursuit of truth knows no bounds, and the revelations of the past can cast a brilliant light on the innovations of the future.

Questions to Ponder…

1.   If the authors of the Bible can write about nuclear bombs during their time of swords, shields and spears, isn't this a clear proof of the sovereignty of God, the God of past, present and future?

2.   Can you think of any explanation why the authors of the Bible would use specific words like "the elements will be destroyed by fire" instead of a general word like "materials"?

3.   What other possible weapons can cause "… their flesh will rot while they are still standing on their feet, their eyes will rot in their sockets, and their tongues will rot in their mouths." Is the Bible describing future biological (the key word used is plague) warfare?

I believe that, based on the above, the Bible is indeed the Word of God. What about you?

☐

Chapter 8: Did the Bible Prophesize About the Internet and the Modern World Technologies?

Chapter 8: Did the Bible Prophesize About the Internet and the Modern World Technologies?

Moses, now well-versed in the incredible advancements of the future, sat across from Einstein in the same cozy coffee shop where their discussions had spanned centuries. This time, it was Moses who had a burning question, and his excitement was palpable. He leaned forward, his eyes shining with curiosity.

"I am puzzled about a verse in the Bible regarding the second coming of Christ. It is stated in Revelation 1:7 that '… every eye will see him' when He next comes back to Earth.

During my times in the ancient days where Christians and Jews were all living within the vicinity of Israel and Judah, if we look up the sky, it is possible that every eye can see Jesus coming down from the sky. But now, during your time, Einstein, Christians and Jews are all scattered around the world. How is this possible that '…every eye will see him…'?" enquired Moses.

"Look, he is coming with the clouds,"

and "every eye will see him,

even those who pierced him";

and all peoples on earth "will mourn because of him." So shall it be! Amen.

Revelation 1:7 NIV

Einstein, always eager to engage in these timeless dialogues, pondered the question. He knew that the answer lay in the profound transformations of the future. "Moses," he began, "what you've stumbled upon is indeed a remarkable prophecy, one that can be understood through the lens of the incredible technologies of the future."

With a thoughtful nod, Moses listened intently as Einstein continued, "In the era to come, humanity will invent something called the 'World Wide Web' or simply 'the Internet.' It will connect people from all corners of the Earth, allowing them to share information, images, and even videos in real time."

Moses' eyes widened with intrigue, trying to fathom such a concept. "Go on," he urged.

Einstein explained further, "Additionally, there will be small, handheld devices called mobile phones equipped with cameras. People will carry these devices with them wherever they go, and these phones will be capable of capturing and broadcasting events as they happen anywhere and everywhere around the world."

Moses absorbed this information, his imagination running wild. "So, you mean that everyone will be able to witness the second coming of Christ around the world?"

Einstein nodded emphatically. "Exactly. With the advent of technologies like Facebook live streaming and YouTube streaming, any momentous event will be instantly shared with the world. When the second coming of Christ occurs, it will be such a sensational event that no one will miss it."

Moses marvelled at the foresight of this prophecy. "It's truly remarkable how the Bible's words transcend time and space," he said, his voice filled with wonder.

Einstein smiled warmly. "Indeed, Moses, and it underscores the enduring power of faith and the human spirit to innovate. The future is filled with mysteries and marvels that bridge the past and the present, and together, we continue to explore the profound connections between science, spirituality, ancient scripture's prophesies and God's plan."

Revelation 1:7 is an ancient prophesy of these modern-day inventions, namely:

1. The Internet or World Wide Web

2. Mobile phones with video cameras

3. Facebook streaming or YouTube streaming or other social media streaming technologies

4. Television and or satellite broadcasting technologies

As they sipped their coffee, Moses and Einstein contemplated the ever-expanding boundaries of human knowledge.

"There is one more verse that puzzles me," Moses said, eager and excited by what he learnt of modern technologies.

"But you, Daniel, roll up and seal the words of the scroll until the time of the end. Many will go here and there to increase knowledge."

Daniel 12:4 NIV

"Moses," Einstein began, "Daniel 12:4 speaks of 'many will go here and there…'. Today, millions of people are travelling at tremendous speed across cities, countries and oceans, covering great distances, all within a few hours. It would have taken weeks and months by your camels and donkeys in your time. You are talking of a **prophesy of modern transportation like airplanes, ships, mass rapid transit, bullet trains, etc!**

'…**to increase knowledge'** is the second part of the prophesy that points to the invention of internet, where tons of information in the form or words, music and videos are made available within a fraction of a second. In today's world, people travel the globe swiftly, seeking knowledge, much as the Bible seems to suggest."

Moses, pondering this notion, nodded slowly. "Indeed, the symbolism is striking. In an age where information is transmitted instantaneously across huge geographical distance, the idea that 'every eye will see' resonates with the concept of a global audience witnessing events unfold in real-time through the internet and social media. It's a testament to the profound ways in which the Bible's messages continue to echo through the ages." "Yes, many, many people are on the move… several millions a day, every day." remarked Einstein.

Moses struggled to imagine how many camels it would take to carry a million people across Israel and how fast the camels would need to run to reach Egypt within a few hours.

As Einstein and Moses delved deeper into these potential prophetic connections, they marvelled at the intricate web of symbolism and metaphors that are weaved throughout the Bible. The Bible invites readers to explore the profound resonance between ancient wisdom and the remarkable technological advancements of our modern age. The journey of discovery continues, revealing how the age-old scriptures continue to inspire contemplation in the digital era.

Chapter 9: The Revelation of a New Journey and a New Life Ahead.

Chapter 9: The Revelation of a New Journey and a New Life Ahead.

What is Revelation?

Revelation, in its essence, is the unveiling of, or the revealing of something previously concealed. In the context of the Bible, in the final book of the Bible, Revelation, God reveals glimpses of the future, both on earth and in heaven, how the world will eventually end and how God will overcome evil.

However, in the context of this book, revelation takes on a different meaning: a summary, a revealing of insights garnered from the preceding chapters and a new perspective on the age-old debate: Who Wins: Science or Scripture?

Let us embark on this concluding chapter as we reflect on the revelations that have emerged from this book, each page shedding a little light on the intricate dance between scripture, science and the timeless wisdom found in sacred scripture. As we journey through the chapters, we encounter questions, ponder over mysteries and seek answers.

Unveiling the Answers:

1. Is the Bible the Word of God?

The Bible is not a science book, yet it is scientifically accurate. It contains amazing scientific facts that were penned thousands of years before modern scientists discovered them. In-depth and evidence-based scientific explanations reveal the greatness and wisdom of God. The Bible aligns with science because scientists prove them so. Many people believe that science is the truth, and if the Bible and science are aligned, then the Bible is the truth.

Do you agree and believe that, based on the arguments, evidence and rational thinking presented throughout this book, the Bible is indeed the Word of God?

Its ability to foresee and prophesize scientific discoveries and momentous events through multiple prophecies, thousands of years ahead accurately, suggests a divine origin.

In the grand tapestry of time, God reigns as the sovereign ruler of the past, the present, and the future. Since He knows and controls the future, He has revealed to us numerous facts and events in the Bible, thousands of years ahead of discoveries by scientists, historians, medical doctors, astronomers, engineers and archologists **so that we may know and believe.**

2.   Is there a sovereign God?

If there is no sovereign God, who created you?

Who balanced the ecosystems harmoniously in this diversified planet? Certainly not the chaotic evolution! Remember that the Theory of Evolution is debunked in Chapter 5.

Who created the flowers and the bees and billions of perfectly created creatures around the planet?

Who told the flowers to bloom all together in spring, all the trees to shed their leaves in autumn, all over the world?

Who told the birds that winter is coming and that they should all fly to warmer countries for a few months, then return home again when winter is over?

Who gave the humble bees their GPS (Global Positioning System) to find their way home to their hives?

Who created the Earth, the Moon, the Sun and all the billion stars?

Who determined that the distance between the earth and the sun is exactly 147.65 million km? If this distance is too near, Earth will be scotched. If it is too far, it will be frozen. How can the Big Bang Theory achieve this perfect distance by mere coincidence?

With this newfound understanding derived from this book, we stand at the crossroad of faith and science. It is not a battle but an invitation to harmonize these seemingly disparate realms, to recognize that the pursuit of truth can encompass both science and spirituality.

Do you agree that, based on the reasonings presented, there is a sovereign God, an intelligent creator, who not only creates the universe, but controls its past, present, and future. He had written the prophesies down and several thousand years later, all of them will come to pass.

3. **More profound questions:** The Bible is written not just for the people of the ancient world; it is especially relevant for people like us living in this 21st century. Else,

>   a.   why would God want to reveal the invention of nuclear bombs to people who fight with swords, shields, and spears?

>   b.   why would God want to reveal inventions of airplanes and bullet trains to people who travel on camels and in carriages?

He reveals all these to us, to you and me, the twentieth century people, so that we can be prepared for Christ's second coming. Yes, Jesus is coming again!

4. **The Call to Seek Truth**

I encourage you, my dear readers, to take this revelation to heart, to be inspired to embark on your own quest for truth. Start by reading the Bible, from cover to cover, with an open heart and mind. Seek understanding, ask questions, and engage in the age-old pursuit of wisdom that has shaped the human journey.

Ask a Christian friend, I am sure they will be glad to hold your hand and guide you.

Or seek a church and talk to someone there to begin your journey.

Drop me an email: johnseah@everesti.com. I am excited to know more about your journey.

Your new journey beckons…your new life awaits.

Conclusion

As we conclude this book, let us remember that the unveiling of truth is a continual ever winding, ever learning and ever questioning journey. It is an ongoing dialogue

between the known and the unknown, the scientific and the spiritual. The questions we raise in these chapters not only provide you with definitive answers, but they also serve as signposts on your quest for a deeper understanding and a more profound transformation.

May this book inspire you to embrace the mysteries of the universe, to seek knowledge with humility and to approach the interplay of science and faith with an open heart. For in the end, it is the journey itself, the quest for truth, which enriches our lives and expands our horizons.

It is important to note that where there is an all-powerful and all-knowing God, there is always room for the supernatural and miracles that science cannot fully explain yet. That should be another journey to discover... another book in the making. While the Bible has documented what God did and explains why he did them, science discovers the evidence that explains them thousands of years later, as and when science's instruments become capable of detecting them. More science and scripture synchronisation will be revealed, in their cosmic waltz.

A new revelation awaits those who dare to seek it - the spiritual realm, which science has yet to comprehend or to invent instruments to probe, to detect and to monitor. This journey of science and scripture continues to unfold in the most wondrous of ways.

While most races are measured in seconds or hundredths of a second, our race in time between science and scripture is measured in terms of hundreds or thousands of years.

May we share with you our answers to the question, "Who wins: Science or Scripture?"

1.   The God of the past, present and future is the Creator of the Universe. He foresaw all the events on Earth, and He inspired a team of biblical writers to record them in the Bible, so that we may believe in Him and be prepared.

2.   Among all books ever written, the Bible is unique in foretelling specific events accurately, centuries before they occur. Hundreds of prophecies appear in the pages of the Bible, most of which have already been fulfilled, with no errors. Fulfilled prophecies are the evidence for the reliability of the Bible.

3.   Perhaps we have to wait for another few thousand years later for science to catch up to invent machines to prove the existence of the spiritual realm scientifically.

Be prepared for what?

1.   Be prepared for the second coming of Christ.

2.   Be prepared for the final days that will end the world.

3.   Be prepared for the big troubles that lie ahead as revealed in Revelation, the final book of the Bible.

Now faith is confidence in what we hope for and assurance about what we do not see.

Hebrews 11:1 NIV

May God bless you!

References, Credits & Bibliography

1.   Ray Comfort, Scientific facts in the Bible 100 facts to believe the Bible is Supernatural in Origin. Bridge-Logos, Inc. 2001, 2020 USA

2.   Dr Michael Guillen, Amazing Truths How science and Bible Agrees. Zondervan, 2015, USA

3.   Henry M. Morris Science and the Bible Revised and expanded Moody Publishers 1986 USA

4.   Gerald L. Schroeder: The science of God The convergence of scientific and biblical wisdom The Free Press, 1997 USA

5.   Chat GPT powered by OpenAI, for generating cover designs and all the images used in this book.

6.   Institute of Creation Research https://www.icr.org/ 1830 Royal Ln, Dallas, TX, 75229

7. David Pawson Website:

    https://davidpawson.org/resources/series/

8. Holy Bible, New International Version®, NIV® Copyright ©1973, 1978, 1984, 2011 by Biblica, Inc.®

9. The Wyatt Family Website: www.ronwyatt.com

a. https://www.ronwyatt.com/noahs_ark_book

b.

https://youtube/PIpvIVLQ2Dk?si=g7NYABATy7KzDEr_
Ron Wyatt Discoveries [2022] Gomorrah, Red Sea Crossing, Mt Sinai, Noah's Ark, Blood of Christ

c. https://www.youtube.com/shorts/R4TMrQ_yDUw New Discovery At Mt Sinai! #ronwyatt #bible #mountsinai #arkofthecovenant #fyp

d. https://www.ronwyatt.com/red_sea_crossing

e. https://www.ronwyatt.com/noahs_ark

About the Author

John Seah, the author of "Who Wins: Science or Scripture?" is a man whose journey from atheism to faith was filled with hesitations, iterations and procrastinations. With a background as an engineer and a deep love for science and technology, John spent a significant portion of his life firmly entrenched in atheism. Questioning about everything, he could not reconcile between science and scripture.

Throughout his career, which included roles as a computer engineer, a regional corporate skills trainer and a business owner, many Christians attempted to share their faith with him. However, none could present a logical and compelling case for the existence of God that could resonate with John's rational mind.

It was only at the age of 55 that John's view of the world underwent a profound transformation. After accepting Christ into his life, he embarks on a conscientious exploration of the Bible. To his amazement, he discovers that the pages of the Scripture are richly infused with scientific and engineering insights. This newfound understanding ignites a passion within him to bridge the gap between science and scripture, seeking to illuminate the rationality of belief without the need for decades of searching.

John graduated with a Master of Science degree in Computer Studies (Artificial Intelligence). Professionally, he is a certified Information Technology Infrastructure Library (ITIL) V3 Expert. John is also a member of the world-wide team of writers for the ITIL V3 Service Strategy manual and a Chartered Engineer (UK). He has also authored two other business books:

- Turning Ideas into Gold: A Practical Guide for Innovators

- Turning Ideas into Profit

John Seah's journey from atheism to Christianity and his subsequent quest to reconcile science and spirituality has culminated in this book. Through his unique perspective and logical approach, he endeavours to shed light on the age-old debate between science and scripture, offering a path for atheists and sceptics to discover the compelling harmony between the two realms. His story serves as a testament to the transformative power of faith and the boundless possibilities that arise when one dares to seek truth with an open mind and an open heart.

www.ingramcontent.com/pod-product-compliance
Lightning Source LLC
Chambersburg PA
CBHW071546150726
48000CB00002B/958